D0899446

SNOW WATER

SNOW WATER

Michael Longley

CAPE POETRY

Published by Jonathan Cape 2004

2 4 6 8 10 9 7 5 3 1

Copyright © Michael Longley 2004

Michael Longley has asserted his right under the Copyright, Designs
and Patents Act 1988 to be identified as the author of this work

First published in Great Britain in 2004 by
Jonathan Cape
Random House, 20 Vauxhall Bridge Road, London SW1V 2SA

Random House Australia (Pty) Limited
20 Alfred Street, Milsons Point, Sydney,
New South Wales 2061, Australia

Random House New Zealand Limited
18 Poland Road, Glenfield,
Auckland 10, New Zealand

Random House South Africa (Pty) Limited
Endulini, 5A Jubilee Road, Parktown 2193, South Africa

The Random House Group Limited Reg. No. 954009
www.randomhouse.co.uk

A CIP catalogue record for this book is available from the British Library

ISBN 0-224-07257-9
ISBN 0-224-07358-3 (Leather bound limited edition)

Papers used by Random House are natural,
recyclable products made from wood grown in sustainable forests;
the manufacturing processes conform to the environmental
regulations of the country of origin

Typeset by Palimpsest Book Production Limited
Polmont, Stirlingshire
Printed and bound in Great Britain by
Biddles Ltd, Guildford & King's Lynn, Norfolk

For David Cabot

Above Caher Island the same cloud hangs
As yesterday, shaped like a sea-horse, the sky
A pink ceiling, the sea a damselfly blue.

The hare sees this as she circles your cottage
Which is just another erratic boulder,
So does the otter stepping out of the waves.

CONTENTS

*. . . the sparks of his father curved
into the west of the lake . . .*
                    − Medbh McGuckian

OVERHEAD

The beech tree looks circular from overhead
With its own little cumulus of exhalations.
Can you spot my skull under the nearby roof,
Its bald patch, the poem-cloud hanging there?

MOON CAKES

The wee transcendental mountain cottage
is where I continue painting almond
and plum blossom into extreme old age
(i.e. late winter, a covering of snow,
the full moon's unattainability
brightening my dilapidated studio);
is where I overdose on jasmine tea and
moon cakes (a complicated recipe).

SNOW WATER

A fastidious brewer of tea, a tea
Connoisseur as well as a poet,
I modestly request on my sixtieth
Birthday a gift of snow water.

Tea steam and ink stains. Single-
Mindedly I scald my teapot and
Measure out some Silver Needles Tea,
Enough for a second steeping.

Other favourites include Clear
Distance and Eyebrows of Longevity
Or, from precarious mountain peaks,
Cloud Mist Tea (quite delectable)

Which competent monkeys harvest
Filling their baskets with choice leaves
And bringing them down to where I wait
With my crock of snow water.

FLIGHT FEATHERS

I

It was I who placed the nest-box under our bedroom
Window and inspired the nuptial flight, flight feathers
Shivering like a moth close to where we snuggle.
This is the blue tits' wheezy epithalamion.

II

I took this down from the electricity line
Where a redwing was recommending *sleep sleep*.
At the lopsided gatepost my only merlin
Was going on about golden plover, wisps of snipe.

III

Will you remember that rainbow in Leitrim low
As the fields, an extra hedge no one had cleared
From the poor land, a long acre no one had drained,
Cover for all of the birds that have disappeared?

IV

The tide-digested burial mound has almost gone.
A peregrine is stooping high above my breastbone.

ABOVE DOOAGHTRY

Where the duach rises to a small plateau
That overlooks the sand dunes from Dooaghtry
To Roonkeel, and just beyond the cottage's
Higgledy perimeter fence-posts
At Carrigskeewaun, bury my ashes,

For the burial mound at Templedoomore
Has been erased by wind and sea, the same
Old stone-age sea that came as far inland
As Cloonaghmanagh and chose the place
That I choose as a promontory, a fort:

Let boulders at the top encircle me,
Neither a drystone wall nor a cairn, space
For the otter to die and the mountain hare
To lick snow stains from her underside,
A table for the peregrine and ravens,

A prickly double-bed as well, nettles
And carline-thistles, a sheeps' wool pillow,
So that, should she decide to join me there,
Our sandy dander to Allaran Point
Or Tonakeera will take for ever.

MARSH MARIGOLDS

in memory of Penny Cabot

Decades ago you showed me marsh marigolds
At Carrigskeewaun and behind a drystone wall
The waterlily lake's harvest of helleborines.

As you lie dying there can be only one lapwing
Immortalising at Dooaghtry your minty
Footsteps around the last of the yellow flags.

PETALWORT

for Michael Viney

You want your ashes to swirl along the strand
At Thallabaun – amongst clockwork, approachable,
Circumambulatory sanderlings, crab shells,
Bladderwrack, phosphorescence at spring tide –

Around the burial mound's wind-and-wave-inspired
Vanishing act – through dowel-holes in the wreck –
Into bottles but without a message, only
Self-effacement in sand, additional eddies.

There's no such place as heaven, so let it be
The Carricknashinnagh shoal or Caher
Island where you honeymooned in a tent
Amid the pilgrim-fishermen's stations,

Your spillet disentangling and trailing off
Into the night, a ghost on every hook – dab
And flounder, thorny skate – at ebb tide you
Kneeling on watery sand to haul them in.

Let us choose for the wreath a flower so small
Even you haven't spotted on the dune-slack
Between Claggan and Lackakeely its rosette –
Petalwort: snail snack, angel's nosegay.

AN OCTOBER SUN

in memory of Michael Hartnett

Something inconsolable in you looks me in the eye,
An October sun flashing off the rainy camber.
And something ironical too, as though we could
Warm our hands at turf stacks along the road.

Good poems are as comfortlessly constructed,
Each sod handled how many times. Michael, your
Poems endure the downpour like the skylark's
Chilly hallelujah, the robin's autumn song.

CEILIDH

A ceilidh at Carrigskeewaun would now include
The ghost of Joe O'Toole at ease on his hummock
The far side of Corragaun Lake as he listens to
The O'Tooles from Inishdeigil who settled here
Eighty years ago, thirteen O'Tooles, each of them
A singer or fiddler, thirteen under the one roof,
A happy family but an unlucky one, Joe says,
And the visitors from Connemara who have rowed
Their currachs across the Killary for the music,
And my ghost at the duach's sheepbitten edge
Keeping an eye on the lamps in the windows here
But distracted by the nervy plover that pretends
A broken wing, by the long-lived oystercatcher
That calls out behind me from Thallabaun Strand.
The thirteen O'Tooles are singing about everything.
Their salty eggs are cherished for miles around.
There's a hazel copse near the lake without a name.
Dog violets, sorrel, wood spurge are growing there.
On Inishdeigil there's a well of the purest water.
Is that Arcturus or a faraway outhouse light?
The crescent moon's a coracle for Venus. Look.
Through the tide and over the Owennadornaun
Are shouldered the coffins of the thirteen O'Tooles.

SHADOWS

I

A flat circle of flat stones, anonymous
Headstones commemorating the burial mound,
The dead suspended in the scenery
At head height roughly, unmoved by the wind:

Just as you and I swimming yesterday
At high tide beyond Allaran Point, now
Would be floundering in mid-air
Between that rock pool and the samphire ridge.

II

Seven hares encircle me and you
(We have counted them playing together)
Not too far from the hermetic snipe,

The otters we haven't seen for years
(Although today we heard one whistling)
Shadows between dragonfly and elver.

ARRIVAL

It is as though David had whitewashed the cottage
And the gateposts in the distance for this moment,
The whooper swans' arrival, with you wide awake
In your white nightdress at the erratic boulder
Counting through binoculars. Oh, what day is it
This October? And how many of them are there?

ECHOES

I

I am describing to you on the phone
Stonechats backlit by an October sunset,
A pair that seems to be flirting in the cold.
I am looking out of the bedroom window.
They fluster along the fuchsia hedge and perch
On bare twigs the wind has stripped for them.

II

As beautiful as bog asphodel in flower
Is bog asphodel in seed. Or nearly.
An echo. Rusty-orange October tones.
This late there are gentians and centaury
And a bumble bee on a thistle head
Suspended, neither feeding nor dying.

III

Forty-two whoopers call, then the echoes
As though there are more swans over the ridge.

AFTER TRA-NA-ROSSAN

You were still far away. I was only the wind
When I wrote in my woolgathering twentieth
Year about an abstract expanse in Donegal:

'We walked on Tra-na-rossan strand;
the Atlantic winds were wiping the heat
from the August sun and the stretching sand
was cold beneath our naked feet;

our prints were washed and covered by the tide:
and so we walked through all our days
until there was too much to hide;
no wind to cool our open ways,

no passing tide to wash the traces
of transgression from the secret places.'

Then we filled the details in: a lapwing's
Reedy sigh above the duach, a tortoiseshell
Hilltopping on the cairn, autumn lady's tresses,
The sandwort-starry path to Carrigskeewaun.

I am looking at you through binoculars
As you open the galvanized aeolian gate
In silence and walk away towards the sea.

SNOW GEESE

So far away as to be almost absent
And yet so many of them we can hear
The line of snow geese along the horizon.
Tell me about cranberry fields, the harvest
Floating on flood water, acres of crimson.

I remember a solitary snow goose
Among smudgy cormorants on the Saltees
Decades ago. Today I calculate
Forty thousand snow geese, and pick for you
From the distance individual cranberries.

THE PATTERN

Thirty-six years, to the day, after our wedding
When a cold figure-revealing wind blew against you
And lifted your veil, I find in its fat envelope
The six-shilling *Vogue* pattern for your bride's dress,
Complicated instructions for stitching bodice
And skirt, box pleats and hems, tissue-paper outlines,
Semblances of skin which I nervously unfold
And hold up in snow light, for snow has been falling
On this windless day, and I glimpse your wedding dress
And white shoes outside in the transformed garden
Where the clothesline and every twig have been covered.

THE SETT

A friend's betrayal of you brings to mind
His anecdote about neighbours in Donegal
Who poured petrol into a badger's sett, that
Underground intelligence not unlike your own
Curling up among the root systems.
                                    Oh, why
Can the badger not have more than one address
Like the otter its hovers at Cloonaghmanagh
And Claggan and Carrigskeewaun, its holt
A glimmering between us at Dooaghtry?
I safeguard a bubble-rosary under ice.

ASCHY

We are both in our sixties now, our bodies
Growing stranger and more vulnerable.
It is time for that tonic called *aschy*,
Shadowy cherry-juice from South Russia.

The Argippaei who are all bald from birth,
Snub-nosed and long-chinned, lap it up
With lipsmacking gusto or mix it with milk
Or make pancakes out of the sediment.

In bitter spells they wrap the trunks with felt
As thick and white as the snowy weather.
A weird sanctity protects you and me
While we stay under our ponticum-tree.

DIPPER

Our only dipper on the Owennadornaun
Delayed us, so that we made it and no more
Through the spring tide, wading up to our waists:
Naked from the navel down, did we appear
Harmless to the golden plovers slow to rise
From their feeding on the waterlogged duach?
Then fire-gazing-and-log-and-turf-arranging
Therapy which should have unfrozen lust but
In the dark flood water a darker knot became
Two heron-unsettling-and-lapwing-lifting
Otters, our first for years at Carrigskeewaun,
And we rationed out binocular moments
Behind the curtains of the bedroom window
And watched them as they unravelled out of view.

STONECHAT

A flicker on the highest twig, a breast
That kindles the last of the fuchsia flowers
And the October sunset still to come
When we face the Carricknashinnagh shoal
And all the islands in a golden backwash
Where sanderlings scurry, two cormorants
Peeking at me and you over breakers
That interrupt the glow, behind us
A rainbow ascending out of Roonkeel
High above Six Noggins, disappearing
Between Mweelrea's crests, and we return
To the white cottage with its fuchsia hedge
To share for a second time the stonechat's
Flirtatious tail and flinty scolding.

ROBIN

A robin is singing from the cottage chimney.
Departure means stepping through the sound-drapes
Of his pessimistic skin-and-bone aubade.
Household chores begin: wiping wet windows
For Venus in greeny solitariness, sky-coin,
Morning's retina; scattering from the wonky
Bucket immaterial ashes over moor grass
Turned suddenly redder at the equinox;
Spreading newspapers by the hearth for blackened
Hailstones. We have slept next to the whoopers'
Nightlong echoing domestic hubbub.
A watery sun-glare is melting them.
His shadow on the lawn betrays the robin.
I would count the swans but it hurts my eyes.

WHEATEAR

Poem Beginning with a Line of J. M. Synge

Brown lark beside the sun
Supervising Carrigskeewaun
In late May, marsh marigolds
And yellow flags, trout at the low
Bridge hesitating, even
The ravens' ramshackle nest –
Applaud yourself, applaud me
As I find inside the cottage
A wheatear from Africa
Banging against the windowpane
And hold in my hands her creamy-
Buff underparts and white rump
And carry her to the door
And she joins you beside the sun
Before skimming across the dunes
To mimic in a rabbit hole
Among silverweed and speedwell
My panic, my breathlessness.

SNIPE

in memory of Sheila Smyth

I wanted it to be a snipe from Belfast Lough's
Mud flats, the nightflier that jooked into my headlights.
It could as well have been a knot or a godwit
From the Arctic, a bar-tailed godwit would you say?
Oh, what amateur ornithologists we are!
I had been out celebrating your life, and now
Here you were flapping into your immortality.
Everyone who loved you remembers how birdlike
Your body and behaviour were, exquisiteness.
I stopped the car and held in my lights the lost bird.
It froze like an illustration, the sensitive
Long beak disinclined to probe the tarmacadam.

TWO PHEASANTS

As though from a catastrophic wedding reception
The cock pheasant in his elaborate waistcoat
Exploded over cultivated ground to where
A car in front of our car had crushed his bride.

I got the picture in no time in my wing-mirror
As in a woodcut by Hokusai who highlighted
The head for me, the white neck-ring and red wattles,
The long coppery tail, the elegance and pain.

HOUSE SPARROWS

The sparrows have quit our house, house sparrows
That cheeped in the gutters, stone-age hangers-on
That splashed in our puddles, dust-bathers.
                                            'Yea,
The sparrow hath found her an house.' But where?

Carthorses are munching oats from their nosebags
At a water trough surrounded by sparrows
That bicker and pick up the falling grains.

PRIMARY COLOURS

When Sarah went out painting in the wind,
A gust blew the palette from her hand
And splattered with primary colours
The footprints of wild animals.

She carried home 'Low Cloud on Mweelrea'
And 'Storm over Lackakeely', leaving
Burnt Umber behind for the mountain hare
And for the otter Ultramarine.

YELLOW BUNGALOW

after Gerard Dillon

A reproduction of your 'Yellow Bungalow'
Hangs in our newfangled kitchen, dream-mirror,
A woman waiting between turf-box and window
For a young man to put away his accordion
And gut five anonymous fish for supper.

She appreciates the disposition of skillet
And kettle on the stovetop, of poker and tongs,
And keeps her distance in her faraway corner
Beside the Atlantic, while he has learned new tunes
And wants to accompany us to another room.

As soon as I've switched the fan-assisted oven on
And opened the bombinating refrigerator
(I've a meal to prepare) I hear bellows wheeze
And fingernails clitter over buttons and keys.
Cooking smells become part of the composition.

DUSK

Poem Beginning with a Line of Ian Hamilton Finlay

Dusk is in the shed
and in the stable
now Rusty has gone
and her glossy knees
that smell of apple
or woodruff have gone
and her blaze has gone.

LOST

my lost lamb lovelier than all the wool

THE LAST FIELD

We who have fought are friends now all the time,
So walk with me to the last field on the farm
Where orchids grow – pyramidal, I confirm –
Under the hawthorn hedge and across the path
From higher-than-head-high maize, a pink wreath
On the limey flat-earth plain of County Meath,
As unexpected as the deadly nightshade
And scarlet pimpernel that hid in maize seed,
Stowaways, outcasts, exquisite beside
The dark green practical uprightness of your crop
(Fodder for cows), then other plants to look up
Later in the flora, but not before we stop
One dragonfly in our memories like a rhyme,
A farm animal from here on, we confirm
Who have fought and are friends now all the time.

THREE BUTTERFLIES

for Fleur Adcock

Your sister in New Zealand held the telephone
Above your mother in her open coffin
For you to communicate. How many times
Did silence encircle the globe before
The peacock butterfly arrived in your room?
We all know what the butterfly represents.
I granted my own mother a cabbage-white.
On the Dooaghtry cairn which commemorates
God knows whom a tortoiseshell alighted
To sun itself. It had been wintering
In memory's outhouse and escaped the wren.

OLD POETS

for Anne Stevenson

Old poets regurgitate
Pellets of chewed-up paper
Packed with shrew tails, frog bones,
Beetle wings, wisdom.

OWL CASES

for Medbh McGuckian

Leaving breath-haze and fingerprints
All over the glass case that contains
Barn-and-steeple familiars, we
Pick out the owl that is all ears,
As though tuning in with its feathers
To the togetherness of our heads.

Let us absorb Bubo bubo's
Hare-splitting claws, and such dark eyes
Above that wavering hoot (you know
The one) which is the voice of God,
And the face shaped like a heart
Or the shriek from a hollow tree.

We overlook the snowy owl
Snowdrifting in its separate case
Where it hunts by day, whose yellow gaze
Follows around the museum
Me and you, my dear, owl-lovers,
Lovers of otherworldliness.

LEVEL PEGGING

for Michael Allen

I

After a whole day shore fishing off Allaran Point
And Tonakeera you brought back one mackerel
Which I cooked with reverence and mustard sauce.
At the stepping stones near the burial mound
I tickled a somnolent salmon to death for you.
We nabbed nothing at all with the butterfly net.

Hunters, gatherers, would-be retiarii
We succeeded at least in entangling ourselves.
When the red Canadian kite became invisible
In Donegal, we fastened the line to a bollard
And sat for hours and looked at people on the pier
Looking up at our sky-dot, fishing in the sky.

II

You were driving my Escort in the Mournes when –
Brake-failure – Robert Lowell and you careered
Downhill: 'Longley's car is a bundle of wounds.'
When his last big poem had done for Hugh MacDiarmid
And he collapsed, we wrapped his dentures in a hanky
And carried them like a relic to the hospital.

We looked after poets after a fashion. And you
Who over the decades in the Crown, the Eglantine,
The Bot, the Wellie, the Chelsea have washed down
Poetry and pottage without splashing a page
And scanned for life-threatening affectation
My latest 'wee poem' – you have looked after me.

I was a booby-trapped corpse in the squaddies' sights.
The arsehole of nowhere. Dawn in a mountainy bog.
From the back seat alcohol fumed as I slumbered
Surrounded by Paras, then – all innocence – you
Turned up with explanations and a petrol can.
They lowered their rifles when I opened my eyes.

Our Stingers-and-Harvey-Wallbangers period
With its plaintive anthem 'The Long and Winding Road'
Was a time of assassinations, tit-for-tat
Terror. You were Ulster's only floating voter, your
Political intelligence a wonky hedgehopping
Bi-plane that looped the loop above the killing fields.

IV

Rubbed out by winds Anaximines imagined,
The burial mound at Templedoomore has gone.
Locals have driven their tractors along the strand
And tugged apart the wooden wreck for gateposts.
There are fewer exits than you'd think, fewer spars
For us to build our ship of death and sail away.

Remember playing cards to the crash of breakers,
Snipe drumming from the estuary, smoky gossip
In Carrigskeewaun about marriages and making wills?
I'll cut if you deal – a last game of cribbage, burnt
Matches our representatives, stick men who race
Slowly round the board with peg legs stuck in the hole.

THE PEAR

for John Montague

Someone has left three oranges and a pear
On Baudelaire's grave. Orchard of headstones.
The pear dangles in memory as from a branch.
Or is it a symbol, a poetic windfall,
A lucky sign? You put it in your pocket.

We have betrayed each other, we agree.
Like Peter, I suggest, not like Judas – no.
I love it when you link your arm with mine.
You eat half the pear and hand the rest to me.
The dead poet forgives the thieves their hunger.

TWO SKUNKS

Why, my dear octogenarian Jewish friend,
Does the menagerie of minuscule glass animals
On top of your tv set not include a skunk?
I have been travelling around in America,
Sleeping in wooden houses with squeaky floors,
Landings hung with pictures of lost relatives,
Professors, stationmasters, wise embroiderers.
Driving along the Delaware my poet-host
Stops to let two wild turkeys cross the road.
Is that a third one dithering behind us?
We wind the car windows up – a freshly
Flattened skunk so pongily alive in death
Even the magpies in the dogwood hesitate.
Later we laugh as a three-legged dachshund
Raises its non-existent limb to piddle
At the only set of traffic lights in town.
Laid out in its cotton-wool-lined golden box
A skunk in the Novelty Store beguiles me.
Dawnlight and birdsong kindle my fourposter.
I swaddle your present in my underclothes
For it is time to pack and leave America.
A cardinal flusters at the bedroom window
Like the soul of a little girl who hands over
All of the red things her short life recalls.
Here, my dear octogenarian Jewish friend,
Is my gift for you, a skunk spun out of glass
And so small as to be almost unbreakable.

PINE MARTEN

That stuffed pine marten in the hotel corridor
Ended up on all fours in nineteen-thirteen
And now is making it across No Man's Land where
A patrol of gamekeepers keeps missing him.

EDWARD THOMAS'S POEM

I

I couldn't make out the minuscule handwriting
In the notebook the size of his palm and crinkled
Like an origami quim by shell-blast that stopped
His pocket watch at death. I couldn't read the poem.

II

From where he lay he could hear the skylark's
Skyward exultation, a chaffinch to his left
Fidgeting among the fallen branches,
Then all the birds of the Western Front.

III

The nature poet turned into a war poet as if
He could cure death with the rub of a dock leaf.

SYCAMORE

The sycamore stumps survived the deadliest gales
To put out new growth, leaves sticky with honeydew
And just enough white wood to make a violin.

This was a way of mending the phonograph record
Broken by the unknown soldier before the Somme
(Fritz Kreisler playing Dvořák's 'Humoresque').

The notes of music twirled like sycamore wings
From farmhouse-sheltering-and-dairy-cooling branches
And carried to all corners of the battlefield.

PIPISTRELLE

They kept him alive for years in warm water,
The soldier who had lost his skin.
                                        At night
He was visited by the wounded bat
He had unfrozen after Passchendaele,

Locking its heels under his forefinger
And whispering into the mousy fur.

Before letting the pipistrelle flicker
Above his summery pool and tipple there,

He spread the wing-hand, elbow to thumb.
The membrane felt like a poppy petal.

THE PAINTERS

John Lavery rescued self-heal from waste ground
At Sailly-Saillisel in nineteen-seventeen, and framed
One oblong flower-head packed with purple flowers
Shaped like hooks, a survivor from the battlefield.

When I shouldered my father's coffin his body
Shifted slyly and farted and joined up again
With rotting corpses, old pals from the trenches.
William Orpen said you couldn't paint the smell.

HARMONICA

A tommy drops his harmonica in No Man's Land.
My dad like old Anaximines breathes in and out
Through the holes and reeds and finds this melody.

Our souls are air. They hold us together. Listen.
A music-hall favourite lasts until the end of time.
My dad is playing it. His breath contains the world.

The wind is playing an orchestra of harmonicas.

THE FRONT

I dreamed I was marching up to the Front to die.
There were thousands of us who were going to die.
From the opposite direction, out of step, breathless,
The dead and wounded came, all younger than my son,
Among them my father who might have been my son.
'What is it like?' I shouted after the family face.
'It's cushy, mate! Cushy!' my father-son replied.

WAR & PEACE

Achilles hunts down Hector like a sparrowhawk
Screeching after a horror-struck collared-dove
That flails just in front of her executioner, so
Hector strains under the walls of Troy to stay alive.
Past the windbent wild fig tree and the lookout
Post they both accelerate away from the town
Along a cart-track as far as double well-heads
That gush into the eddying Scamander, in one
Warm water steaming like smoke from a bonfire,
The other running cold as hailstones, snow water,
Handy for the laundry-cisterns carved out of stone
Where Trojan housewives and their pretty daughters
Used to rinse glistening clothes in the good old days,
On washdays before the Greek soldiers came to Troy.

Zeus the cloud-gatherer said to sunny Apollo:
'Sponge the congealed blood from Sarpedon's corpse,
Take him far away from here, out of the line of fire,
Wash him properly in a stream, in running water,
And rub supernatural preservative over him
And wrap him up in imperishable fabrics,
Then hand him over to those speedy chaperons,
Sleep and his twin brother Death, who will bring him
In no time at all to Lycia's abundant farmland
Where his family will bury him with grave-mound
And grave-stone, the entitlement of the dead.'
And Apollo did exactly as he was told:
He carried Sarpedon out of the line of fire,
Washed him properly in a stream, in running water,
And rubbed supernatural preservative over him
And wrapped him up in imperishable fabrics
And handed him over to the speedy chaperons,
Sleep and his twin brother Death, who brought him
In no time at all to Lycia's abundant farmland.

INTERVIEW

'No one has ever lived a luckier life than you,
Achilles, nor ever will: when you were alive
We looked up to you as one of the gods, and now
As a resident down here you dominate the dead.'

'Not even you can make me love death, Odysseus:
I'd far rather clean out ditches on starvation
Wages for some nonentity of a smallholder
Than lord it over the debilitated dead.'

THE MINER

How many of my relatives worked down the mine?
The page of William Longley of Ryhope Colliery
In the Durham Miners' Book of Remembrance
Coincides with my short visit to the cathedral.
Let him who 'breaketh open a shaft' rub shoulders
With the carpenters and blacksmiths and wood-reeves
And gamekeepers and horsehair-curlers whose names
And professions and parentheses I know about
Because they influenced my self-centred make-up
And lived and worked in this other country long ago.
When they turn the page tomorrow, William Longley
Will disappear back into darkness and danger
And crawl on hands and knees in the crypt of the world
Under houses and outhouses and workshops and fields.

IN NOTRE-DAME

When I go back into the cathedral to check
If the candle I lit for you is still burning,
I encounter Job squatting on his dunghill
(Can those be cowrie-shell fossils in the stone?
No. Imagine imagining and carving turds
At eye-level for our sorry edification!)
Such tiny figures make my own body feel huge
And fleshy and hopeless inside the doorway.
In my voice-box the penitents and pickpockets
Murmuring in hundreds down the aisles find room.
Each mouth is a cathedral for the God-crumbs.
Where is the holy water, the snow water for Job?
All of our eyes are broken rose windows.
Your candle singes the eyelashes of morning.

A NORWEGIAN WEDDING

Because the Leprosy Museum is still closed
We find ourselves in St Olaf's, eavesdropping
On a Norwegian wedding. The Lutheran light
Picks us out from among the small congregation.
How few friends anyone has. I'm glad we came.
Christ holds his hands up high above the lovers
And fits his death into the narrow window. Oh,
His sore hands. How many friends does a leper have?
Bride and bridegroom walk past us and into the rain.
It is mid-May. All of the roads out of Bergen
Are bordered with lady's smock and wood anemones.

MONTALE'S DOVE

He writes about a dove that flies away from him
Between the pillars of Ely Cathedral – wing
Clatter and aphrodisiac burbling as well as
Sepulchral knick-knack – a lover's soul escaping.

After a life-time of honey-coloured sunlight
He craves darkness – not death exactly but a nest
Perhaps, a hole in the religious masonry
For resurrection under a smouldering breast.

He doesn't mention how the stained-glass windows
Make walls a momentary rainbow patchwork if
The sun is shining: instead he lets one white feather
Drift among terrible faces up in the roof.

UP THERE

after Giovanni Pascoli

The skylark far away up there in dawnlight
Sky-wanders: arias fall on the farmhouse
While smoke sways raggedly this way and that.

Far away up there the tiny eye takes in
Furrows rolling over in brown munificence
Behind converging teams of white oxen.

A particular sod on black soggy land
Flashes in sunlight like a mirror fragment:
The philosophical labourer binding sheaves
Cocks an ear for the cuckoo's recitatives.

THE LIZARD

At the last restaurant on the road to Pisa airport
The only thing under the pergola to distract me
From gnocchi stuffed with walnuts in porcini sauce
Was a greeny lizard curving her belly like a bowl
So that when she tucked her hind legs behind her
In philosophical fashion and lifted up her hands
As though at prayer or in heated *conversazione*,
She wouldn't scorch her elegant fingers or toes
On the baking concrete and would feel the noon
As no more than a hot buckle securing her eggs.
We left the restaurant on the road to Pisa airport
And flew between Mont Blanc and the Matterhorn.
His lady co-pilot, the captain of our Boeing
Coyly let us know, specialised in smooth landings.

TAXONOMY

Poets used to measure with a half-crown baby toads
Just this size, and bring to life their vague muck-colour.
Ten years ago I counted glow-worms at the waterfall.
Into the puddle that was the salamanders' pool
A dragonfly inserts her long bum and lays eggs.
I have fitted a hundred wing-glints into this one line.

IRISH HARE

Amid São Paulo's endless higgledy concrete
I found in a dream your form again, but woven
Out of banana leaf and Brazilian silence
By the Wayana Indians, as though to last.

WOODEN HARE

Sarah drew a hare under a sky full of large stars
When she was ten: now, more than a childhood later,
In antique Paraty where the sea seeps up the street
Depositing between boulder-sized cobbles sand
And the feathers of snowy egrets and frigate birds,
We meet the hare again, an 'indigenous artefact',
And want to know everything about the animal,
Its crouching body carved out of caxeto, ears
Slotted into the skull, the unexpected markings
(Blotches of butum oil) that represent leaf-shadows
Or are they stars fallen through the forest canopy?
Dare we buy it and bring it back home to Ireland,
The hare in Sarah's picture, the Mato Grosso hare?
Its eyes are made from beeswax and mother-of-pearl.

EARTHSHINE

The Indian boy has blackened his face
As though to imitate the sun's eclipse
Or the moon's, or the forest's shadowiness:
For me he means earthshine, earthlight
Faintly illuminating the crescent moon's
Unsunlit surface: his lips and his eyes
Are watery glimmers and his headdress
An irradiation of white heron feathers.

WOODSMOKE

for Helen Denerley

I

I have just arrived and hesitate between
Water-sounds and your metallic menagerie.
I am lost among the pheasants' heather stands.
A kestrel stoops as though you put him there
With the buzzards high on their thermals criss-
Crossing. Translations, Helen, metaphors.
The mare and stag you made from scrap metal
Are moving in slow motion across your land.
You filled the mare with air and the millennium.
The stag that flashes antlers and pizzle
Was conceived once you spotted in your heap
A tongue for him, a cobbler's last: his tail
Is another cobbler's last. Clashnettie means
(You think) the hollow of the juniper tree.

II

Among the pourers of the molten iron
Were the threatened and bereaved, disguised
In helmets and leather aprons, balancing
Buckets of terror as the furnace roared.
The Deskry's meander does not require
An iron bridge: you and your friends put up
A black rainbow, a darkbow to reflect
The moonbow that shone the January night
A neighbour's two boys were burnt alive,
A whitebow of snow and frost and moonlight
Supporting your cast-iron fourteen-foot span
Across the shallow water, snow water,
From soggy pasture to where the rainbow ends,
Just there, among ragged robin and harebells.

You wanted the kiln to look like a cairn,
A hikers' and lovers' accumulation,
But inside is a clay-lined, bottle-shaped
Emptiness, a hole for the rainwater
And our pebbles. Can you hear them falling?
Whereabouts in your workshop at Clashnettie
Are the leather aprons and gaiters, the boots
With steel toecaps that glint in the moonlight?
Fire splashing over into Deskry Water
Made pocketfuls of accidental sculpture
For children from the glen. Smoke and steam.
You have left a scrap-iron golden eagle
On a boulder up the slopes of Morven
Where he rests in gales near a picnic hut.

IV

You pictured a heron feeding her mate
Or sipping at her own reflection, two
Heads, the bridge's arc, rainbow's template.
It took ten tappings from the sparky kiln.
I picture a heron beneath the bridge
Or, where the boys lie buried, a motionless
Graveside sentinel waiting for ever
To regurgitate field-mouse and water-vole.
What bits and pieces would make a heron?
You put to use for the golden eagle's wings
Tines from a harrow so rusted away
A horse drew it once, or the first tractor.
I am looking for a heron's feather,
A crown-feather preferably, a black one.

You take me to someone else's barbecue,
Strangers gazing at a bonfire, catherine
Wheels and roman candles among the pines
And, as though I am remembering it,
The scent of woodruff under woodsmoke.
Are there people here who are not your friends?
A mother who doesn't understand, a sister?
I am with you. From among the shadowy
Mystifying voices I pick out yours.
We have to imagine one another
Quickly, and then go home, I to the town,
Clothes reeking of smoke and uneasiness,
You to your acre, the dark plantation,
The stream, the dipper bobbing on his stone.

HELEN'S MONKEY

You saw the exhaust and inlet ports as ears,
The hole for measuring Top Dead Centre
(Piston-timing) as a nose, making the eyes
Valve-inspection covers (no longer there).
It took time, Helen, for the monkey's skull
(The cylinder head from a twenties Blackburn)
To find a body: it sat on the windowsill
Through a long evolutionary autumn
Until you came across the unimaginable –
The frame of a motorbike (and a side-car's)
Hidden by snow and heather up a hill
Near Ullapool, a twenties Blackburn of course,
Skeleton recognising skull, and soul
A monkey's soul amalgamated with yours.

PRAXILLA

Sunlight strews leaf-shadows on the kitchen floor.
Is it the beech tree or the basil plant or both?
Praxilla was *not* 'feeble-minded' to have Adonis
Answer that questionnaire in the underworld:
'Sunlight's the most beautiful thing I leave behind,
Then the shimmering stars and the moon's face,
Also ripe cucumbers and apples and pears.'
She is helping me unpack these plastic bags.
I subsist on fragments and improvisations.
Lysippus made a bronze statue of Praxilla
Who 'said nothing worthwhile in her poetry'
And set her groceries alongside the sun and moon.

CORINNA

Have you fallen asleep for ever, Corinna?
In the past you were never the one to lie in.

THE GROUP

I

With Ion of Chios, the prize-winning poet
Who specialises in astronomical phenomena
And the invention of compound adjectives,
I hang around for the sun's white-winged
Forerunner, the air-wandering dawn-star
(And for the splashing-out of good wine).

II

Lamprocles, the dithyrambic poet,
Says the ethereal Pleiades share
The same nomenclature as wood-pigeons.
I must ask him what he makes of that.

III

Myrtis, lyrical poetess from Anthedon,
Craftswoman of a few immortal lines
(A voice like a skylark on a good day)
Overdoes things a bit and goes in for
The same poetry competition as Pindar.

IV

Hypochondriacal Telesilla
For the sake of her health takes up singing
And playing the lyre and gets well enough
To volunteer and man the battlements,
Female defeating male and inspiring
Argos, her hometown, with poetry.

V

Devoutly we coldshoulder Diagoras
For blowing the whistle (in poem and dance)
On the Eleusinian Mysteries: also,
There's a talent of silver for his killer.

VI

A certain person boozes and gorges
And says scandalous things about us all,
Punching the air, 'I've plenty of blows left
If anyone wants to take me on,' he bawls.
The Group would be far better off without
Timocreon of Rhodes (poet, pentathlete).

VII

Oblivious to being out of date,
Which of us will not appear as dopey
As Charixenna, oldfashioned pipe-player
And composer of oldfashioned tunes
And, according to some, a poet too?

WHITE WATER

in memory of James Simmons

Jimmy, you isolated yourself
At the last bend before white water.
We should have been fat jolly poets
In some oriental print who float
Cups of warm saké to one another
On the river, and launch in paper boats
Their poems. We are all separated.
Your abandoned bivouac should be called
Something like the Orchid Pavilion.

HERON

in memory of Kenneth Koch

You died the day I was driving to Carrigskeewaun
(A remote townland in County Mayo, I explain,
Meaning, so far as I know, The Rock of the Wall Fern)
And although it was the wettest Irish year I got the car
Across the river and through the tide with groceries
And laundry for my fortnight among the waterbirds.
If I'd known you were dying, Kenneth, I'd have packed
Into cardboard boxes all your plays and poems as well
And added to curlew and lapwing anxiety-calls
The lyric intensity of your New York Jewish laughter.
You would have loved the sandy drive over the duach
('The what?'), over the machair ('the what?'), the drive
Through the white gateposts and the galvanized gate
Tied with red string, the starlings' sleeping quarters,
The drive towards turf-fired hilarity and disbelief,
'Where are all those otters, Longley, and all those hares?
I see only sparrows here and house sparrows at that!'
You are so tall and skinny I shall conscript a heron
To watch over you on hang-glider wings, old soldier,
An ashy heron, *ardea cinerea*, I remind you
(A pedant neither smallminded nor halfhearted):
'And *cinerarius*?': a slave who heats the iron tongs
In hot ashes for the hair-dresser, a hair-curler
Who will look after every hair on your curly head.
That afternoon was your night-season. I didn't know.
I didn't know that you were 'poured out like water
And all your bones were out of joint'. I didn't know.
Tuck your head in like a heron and trail behind you
Your long legs, take to the air above a townland
That encloses Carrigskeewaun and Central Park.

LEAVES

Is this my final phase? Some of the poems depend
Peaceably like the brown leaves on a sheltered branch.
Others are hanging on through the equinoctial gales
To catch the westering sun's red declension.
I'm thinking of the huge beech tree in our garden.
I can imagine foliage on fire like that.

NOTES & ACKNOWLEDGEMENTS

A few words may require a gloss: *machair* is Irish and
Scots Gaelic for a sandy plain found behind dunes and
affording some pasturage: *duach*, the Irish for sandbanks or
dunes, means in Mayo the same as *machair; dander* is Scots
(or Ulster Scots) for a stroll; *hover* is an otter's temporary
resting place, *holt* its den.

'Snow Geese' is set in the Reifel Migratory Bird
Sanctuary in British Columbia. 'Level Pegging' was
written specially for *Last Before America: Irish and American
Writing: Essays in honour of Michael Allen*, edited by Fran
Brearton and Eamonn Hughes (Blackstaff Press, 2001);
'Old Poets' for *The Way You Say The World: A Celebration
for Anne Stevenson*, compiled by John Lucas and Matt
Simpson (Shoestring Press, 2003). 'Yellow Bungalow' was
written to accompany a reproduction of the painting of
that name by Gerard Dillon in the anthology *Conversation
Piece*, edited by Adrian Rice and Angela Reid (Ulster
Museum/Abbey Press, 2002).

Seven of the poems appeared with work from my earlier
collections in *Cenotaph of Snow: Sixty Poems about War*, a
chapbook published in March 2002 by Stephen Stuart-
Smith at the Enitharmon Press.

Acknowledgements are due to the following publications:
*Carolina Quarterly, Colby Review, College Green, Dublin Review,
Fortnight, Grand Street, Honest Ulsterman, Irish Pages, Irish
Review, Irish Times, London Review of Books, Metre, New
Yorker, Oxford Poetry, Ploughshares, Poetry International, Poetry
Review, Thumbscrew, Times Literary Supplement*, and to the
BBC and RTE.

feathers on water
a snowfall of swans
snow water